Working Women
of the Bible
study guide

4WORDWOMEN.ORG

To order additional copies of this resource:

Order online at 4wordwomen.org or email hello@4wordwomen.org

 4word

To connect, lead and support professional Christian women to achieve their God-given potential.

In numbers far exceeding past generations, women today are earning advanced degrees and entering full-time careers while juggling relationships, families, church and community activities.

71% *of women with children under 18 are working outside the home.*

Professional women - single or married, parenting or not - must navigate a changed business culture that prizes intense career commitment over other priorities.

27% *of professional women are leaving church, feeling underutilized and isolated.*

With a scarcity of female mentors to model professional success balanced with integrated faith and healthy relationships, women are working in survival mode and dropping out of church in record numbers.

The only national organization serving professional Christian women, 4word is narrowing the gap in resources facing every woman serious about her career, relationships and faith.

connect busy working women face to face in local group gatherings, and in an active online community. The 4word: Mentor Program connects women across the nation for mentoring with our proprietary curriculum.

lead today's professional women seeking balance while developing gifts with enormous potential to impact their families, companies, and church communities. The vision is cast in *Work, Love, Pray*, released in 2011 by business and mentoring thought leader Diane Paddison.

support with practical resources: outstanding digital content, inspiring interviews, and a curated resource directory at 4wordwomen.org. Partnerships with more than 200 like-minded organizations leverage our collective impact.

CONTENTS

When I graduated from law school 20 years ago, I wrestled hard with my decision to pursue a fast-paced legal career. I looked around, but I just couldn't seem to find any like-minded women who were passionate about their careers and their faith. Was something wrong with me? Was I wrong to think that God could delight in the pursuit of excellence in a secular and complex world?

It's hard to believe that was 20 years ago. I'd like to think I'm older and wiser, but I still have my share of questions. As a wife, mother, lawyer, author, sister, daughter, and friend, I often feel like I wear too many hats. My journey is about daycare and multitasking, about sacrificed sleep, juggled chores, dueling calendars...but also about faith and joy and love. In fact, I even wrote a book about it called *Chasing Superwoman*. Yet after I wrote my own story - the story of a too-busy mom, wife, and lawyer trying to do it all - I needed to look outside of myself. So I turned to the women of the Bible.

The women of the Bible are incredible mentors. And they tell some amazing stories. Like many women today, the women of the Bible were trying to do it all: providing for their families, caring for the elderly, exercising spiritual leadership. Trying to be strong. Trying to figure out whether God can still use our work, despite our mistakes.

As I meet young women in the marketplace, I often learn that they feel alone and overwhelmed. They too wonder if God really cares about their work; they too are seeking mentors and asking hard questions. They too are asking if the Bible can really provide workable solutions for a fast-paced modern world.

If you are one of these women, I invite you to join me. Let's put one foot in front of us and see what we have in common with the working women of the Bible. My prayer is that in reading their stories, we would find our stories. That we would know how much God values us as working women and how much He values our work.

Are you ready to meet some amazing women?

Susan DiMickele

4word

To the woman that encourages and inspires me,

Welcome to the "Working Women of the Bible Study Guide". Our heart behind this study guide is for you to grow in community with other women. When I have gathered in community with women in my place of caring about God's use of me in relationships and at work, I have been able to support and encourage others as I have gone through this study and through life. I hope it does the same for you.

On page 3, we outline the mission and strategy of 4word: to connect, lead and support professional Christian women to achieve their God-given potential. You can join us online at 4wordwomen.org and through our Local Groups that meet in cities across the country. Women throughout the world have been touched as follows:

"With 4word I experience lots of different kinds of community, but the most beneficial aspect for me has been finding a group of about 10 women who I have created really strong intentional bonds with. We meet twice a week together and have been able to really hear people's stories and their struggles. They understand where I'm at, including my struggles at work and my struggles in my relationships, and also my struggles with trying to grow in my faith. I don't have to hide any part of my life. I don't have to make anything smaller or minimize anything, I can just be me." – Maria, Portland

"What has probably been the most beneficial for me is that I recently found your 4word organization. I have thoroughly enjoyed the emails, blogs, article links, etc. They have been quite encouraging and are great reminders as to how Christ can and should infiltrate our lives in all aspects – whether at home or at work." – Lisa, Dallas

Again, I hope you find a wonderful group of women who you can trust and build authentic relationships with as you go through this study guide.

May you be blessed,

Diane Paddison

Founder, 4word

We're so thrilled you've picked up this study guide as a companion to Susan's amazing book, "Working Women of the Bible." As working women, it is easy to get overwhelmed and forget that God has placed us in our roles. Studying the various working women from the Bible reminds us that we are not the first women to balance work, family, and faith.

I was raised by hard-working parents in South Louisiana. When I landed my dream job out of college, I tried to work harder than everyone else, had no hobbies, and tirelessly strived for achievement at all costs. After a steep climb up the corporate ladder with the "no pets, no plants" rule, I had everything I thought I had ever wanted. I now realize that I spent years putting on masks, labels, and layers to cover up who I really was.....a small town girl raised with chickens, tractors, hand-me-down clothes, and the insecurity that I was never good enough. I had layered on degrees, job titles, stuff, awards, and more stuff to portray an image that I thought the world wanted to see.

While I stood on a Manhattan street on 9/11, I realized the title on my business card and the number of digits on my paycheck did not matter at all. After that day, those layers began to fall off. Some quickly but some slow and painfully. What emerged was a young peacock who was proud of who she was and her differences. She wasn't a penguin who worked hard to dress, talk, walk, and dream like others just to fit into their club. Vulnerability was no longer a bad thing. I let others in, and I liked it.

Since then, I have gotten married, survived cancer, and faced the challenges of infertility and the subsequent losses that followed. Jeff and I have now been married 10 years and have three amazing children that are the light of my life. Before I read the book, I felt very alone in my career pursuits and attempts to juggle being a mother, wife, daughter, sister, and friend. When we are in the thick of the fray, we often feel we are isolated. Once I read the book, I realized there are a lot of us out there whose calling is to work OUTSIDE of the home while still RUNNING the home.

I have learned that you don't have to go through all the yucky things in search of what the world calls success. The world's definition of success will not satisfy. Authenticity and transparency, with yourself and others, are the two of the most important things in life. Being genuine and vulnerable will open the door to meaningful relationships and a meaningful life...and YOUR definition of success will become apparent.

I sincerely hope, in any small way, that this study guide helps you see that God has created you as a working woman and helps you be the amazing you that the Lord created you to be.

With love and support,

Sandra Crawford Williamson, 4word COO

How to Use This Study Guide

:: Individual Study

Read each chapter of Working Women of the Bible and then answer the questions in this study guide. Dig deeper with the Scriptures and prayer prompts that accompany each chapter.

:: Small Groups

Before each meeting, read the chapter of Working Women of the Bible. Go through the questions in the guide and be prepared to discuss and answer the questions with your group. When you meet together, read the Scriptures for the chapter, discuss and answer the questions, and pray through the prayer prompts at the end of the chapter.

:: Large Groups

Before each meeting, read the chapter of Working Women of the Bible and answer the questions for the chapter. When you meet together, read the Scriptures for the chapter, discuss the chapter and your answers to the questions, and pray through the prayer prompts with each other.

While this study guide can be used on your own, we suggest using it in a group setting. It is important to have community with other women where you can support and encourage one another.

When using this study guide in a group setting, remember to practice confidentiality, be authentic, show grace and forgiveness to one another, and respect each other's opinions. Don't try to give advice unless someone asks for it, but always ask good questions!

If you are using this guide with a small group, let us know at hello@4wordwomen.org! You can get ongoing content suggestions, and we can add you to our email list for blogs and other materials.

REFLECT

Before reading this chapter, what words would you have used to describe Eve?

READ

:: Genesis 1-3

:: Colossians 3:23

:: Philippians 1:6

:: Ephesians 2:10

:: 2 Corinthians 9:8

:: Colossians 1:10

After reading this chapter, what words would you use to describe Eve?

Has your perspective of Eve and her life changed? How?

Oftentimes, the translation of the word Ezer is glossed over as meaning only "helper." However, the author points out that word Ezer implies strength, leadership, partnership, and most importantly, work. How does this understanding of the word Ezer change the way you view your work and your purpose as a woman?

How would you characterize your work? How do you feel when you think about your work?

What is good about your daily work?

What can you do that is valuable for those around you?

What can you do for a greater purpose?

Read Colossians 3:23. What would it look like if you approached your work as if you were working for the Lord?

When you mess something up, how do you respond? How did Eve respond?

How can you change the way you face the moments
when you mess up?

Where has your work gone wrong?

Have you ever found yourself in an unbearable job? If so,
how did you respond? What did you learn?

What advice would you give to Kate? Do you know
someone who can identify with her plight? How can we
avoid finding ourselves in her shoes?

How does Eve give us hope for the future? What if God took something you have blown at work – your mistakes and failures – and used it for a greater purpose and plan?

In your life, how have you seen God work good things out of your messy moments?

PRAY

:: Ask God to reveal to you what is good about your work.

:: Ask God to remind you of the value of your work especially on difficult days.

:: Ask God for grace in the moments when you mess up, and ask Him to work through your missteps for His glory.

:: Share your current struggles with God and ask for His guidance as you navigate these struggles.

NOTES

REFLECT

Can you relate to the multiple hats worn by Rahab? Which hat do you most relate to?

What hats do you wear in your own life?

Rahab was often defined by her profession, but she did not let that limit her. Do you find yourself defined by your job title? Do you let that title limit you or do you allow yourself to embrace all of who you are, including your talents, hopes, and dreams?

READ

:: Joshua 2 and 6

:: Joshua 2:11

:: Hebrews 11:1, 31

:: James 2:25

:: Matthew 1:1-17

:: Romans 5:8

:: 2 Corinthians 5:7

Have you ever felt stuck in a job or trapped by your circumstances? If so, how did you respond to that situation?

What can you learn from Rahab about how to handle these situations?

Rahab longed for change in her life. Is there a change you need or hope for in your own life?

NOTES

The author outlines the three R's. The first is readiness. This involves "moving beyond our circumstances and engaging in action. It involves anticipation and preparation." Are you ready for change when God brings it? Ask yourself, "If God acted swiftly and powerfully in my life right now, would I even be ready?" How can you prepare yourself for change in your life?

The second R is risk. Rahab didn't wait for everything to be perfect before she took a risk. She took the risk while completely trusting in God. Are you willing to take the risk to see the change in your life? What is causing you to hesitate?

Has there been a time in your life where you took a risk and found the change you needed?

The third R is regret. You cannot hold onto the past and allow it to define you or keep you from moving forward. Are there any regrets you hold onto that are preventing you from moving forward? How can you let go of these regrets?

Read Ephesians 3:20. What does this verse mean to a woman who is just trying to survive? What impact does it make to know that God wants to give us so much more?

The author points out that God used Rahab when she was still a prostitute. She says that, "it's not about who she is or where she's been, it's about who God is and where he is taking her." How can this truth encourage you in your current situation? How has God already worked in your life, regardless of your situation or status?

NOTES

Do you know a woman who needs a second chance? If so, commit to share Rahab's story with her.

PRAY

:: Tell God about the situations and circumstances that seem to trap you.

:: Ask God to lead you beyond those circumstances as you pursue His plan for you.

:: Ask God to help you implement the three R's in your life.

:: Ask God to help you let go of your regrets that hold you back.

:: Ask God to reveal His plan for you even when you feel hopeless.

4 Ways to Make a Difference in the Life of a Woman Who Needs a Second Chance

NOTES

:: Pray for her and her current circumstances.

:: Encourage her with positive words through notes or phone calls.

:: Affirm her gifts and talents that she might be pushing aside.

:: Be available if she needs a friend to talk to. A listening ear can make a world of difference.

NOTES

NOTES

4word

REFLECT

Do you think Deborah set out to be a judge? By starting small, how does she build her credibility as a leader?

:: Judges 4-5

:: Joshua 1:9

:: Proverbs 31:25

:: Jeremiah 17:7

As Deborah starts small at home, God trains her through everything she does. Reflect on your own life. When has God trained you for your future when you weren't aware that He was preparing you?

The Bible doesn't speak of Deborah's critics. Yet, given her unprecedented leadership, we can imagine resistance to her authority. How do you think Deborah dealt with critics?

How do you handle critics that resist your efforts and promotions in the workplace?

God asked Deborah to put her neck on the line by going into battle. What can we learn from how Deborah handled this frightening challenge?

Has God ever asked you to put your neck on the line? If so, how did you respond?

Barak was scared of going into battle and looked to Deborah for confidence. How did she deal with Barak's lack of confidence? What lessons can you learn from the way Deborah handled Barak's fears?

How can you apply these lessons in the workplace?

Do you agree that women in leadership either don't want to start small or don't want to go big? Which barrier do you most relate to?

4word™

PRAY

NOTES

:: Ask God to prepare you and equip you for the leadership positions He gives you.

:: Ask God for guidance in how you handle your critics.

:: Ask God to give you confidence and the ability to help instill confidence in those around you.

4 Ways to Handle Your Critics in the Workplace

It can be discouraging and frustrating to deal with critics at work. Here are some constructive ways to handle those critics.

:: Pray for your critics. You never know what they might be dealing with outside of work.

:: When their words and resistance are overwhelming, take a step back. It is easy to take it personally, but don't let their criticism impact the great work that you have been called to do.

:: Ask God to remind you of your purpose and the reason He has placed you in your position.

:: Focus on your supporters and the positive impact they have on your work.

NOTES

4word™

REFLECT

Ruth's situation is one where everything seems to have gone wrong. Have you experienced a time in your life where everything went wrong? What were your options? How did you handle your situation?

READ

:: Book of Ruth

:: Ruth 1:16

:: Acts 22:17-21

:: Ephesians 2:10

:: Ruth 2:12

:: Proverbs 14:14

:: Ephesians 6:8

How do you respond when Plan A falls apart? Have you ever embraced Plan C?

How do you decide between a logical Plan B and the illogical Plan C? What would you have done if you were in Ruth's shoes?

Naomi gave up hope and changed her name to Mara, meaning "bitter." How did Ruth respond to Naomi's sadness?

How do you respond when those around you give up? How can you change the way you respond to others' negativity?

Do you struggle doing work that is "beneath" you or seems unimportant? Have you felt that God has forgotten about your resume?

How can you stay positive and be a good, committed worker when you feel your work is unimportant?

Even Paul faced a task that God had called him to but didn't match his qualifications. Have you ever been in a position that didn't match your qualifications? How did you approach your work?

What lessons did you learn through working in that position?

Have you ever been rewarded for your hard work? Think beyond official recognition or promotions. Consider blessings that have arisen as a result of your work.

Notice how Ruth gave up everything yet gained even more. Read Matthew 16:25. How does this verse apply to Ruth?

Consider Boaz's job of overseeing the vineyard. He used his position to be a blessing. How can you use your position to extend grace and bless others?

When you feel stuck in a position, do you lose hope of moving up or out? Or do you look for God's provision and redemption?

Whose work can you relate to the most: Ruth, Boaz, or Naomi? Why? Notice how God uses each of us in different ways to accomplish his plan.

PRAY

:: Ask God to help you work diligently no matter what your job is. Glorify Him through your hard work.

:: Ask God to guide your steps and decisions as you look at options in your life.

:: When you feel stuck, ask God for renewed hope and redemption from your situation.

:: Ask God to help identify people around you who need grace and blessings that you can offer.

5 Ways to Stay Positive When Your Work is Difficult or Feels Unimportant

NOTES

:: Remember that God has called you to your current position. He has a purpose behind it even when you cannot see it.

:: Examine the small things you do in your work and consider the impact those tasks have. Even the seemingly unimportant tasks can make the biggest difference for your company, clients, and coworkers.

:: Smile. When work is overwhelming or frustrating, find a reason to smile. Who knows, maybe one smile will brighten the day of your coworkers who feel the same way that you do.

:: Pray that God will transform your attitude towards your work.

:: Thank God for giving you your work.

NOTES

REFLECT

In your own life, have you experienced the temptations that power brings?

Why do you think Jezebel continued to defy God even after seeing His great power on display?

Jezebel had the right components to be a leader. She had talent, courage, intelligence, and opportunity, but she didn't use them for good. What talents and gifts have you been given?

READ

:: 1 Kings 16:29-19:18

:: 2 Kings 9

:: Proverbs 2:21-22

:: Proverbs 4:14-19

:: Proverbs 10:28-30

:: John 15:1-6

:: Colossians 3:17, 23

How are you using them? Are you glorifying God through the use of your gifts?

Can you think of a modern-day counterpart to Jezebel? Do you think she ever contemplated using her position for good?

The author writes that "it's not really possible to separate our spiritual life from our daily work. Nor is it advisable. Our hearts determine our actions." Have you ever tried to keep your spiritual life separate from your work? How did that work out? How did that affect your spiritual life?

How did that affect your work life?

NOTES

Compare Jezebel's plight with the widow of Sidon. What are their differences? What are their similarities?

Have you reached a crossroads in your life where you feel that God is urging you to change direction? What can you learn from the widow of Sidon? From Jezebel?

Are you afraid to let go of control? What is preventing you from giving God control?

"History shows us that position and power can be the very things that keep us from giving God full reign, especially when it comes to our work." Are you letting God have full reign of your work?

What steps can you take to let go of your control and let God take control?

4word™

PRAY

:: Thank God for the gifts and talents He has given you and ask Him to help you use them for His purposes and glory.

:: Ask God to help you fully surrender to Him.

:: Ask God to help you let go of control and offer it up to Him.

:: Ask God to work through you in all aspects of your life.

NOTES

4word

REFLECT

Do you agree that most of us are harder on women when it comes to reputations? Why?

Who are some modern-day women with desirable reputations?

Have you or someone close to you weathered a reputational challenge? What did you learn in the process?

READ

:: 2 Kings 22

:: James 1:2-4

:: 1 Peter 5:6

:: Colossians 2:6-7

:: Colossians 1:9-11

Josiah did not exclude Huldah because she was a woman. Her qualities and reputation made her stand out. What qualities have you seen in other women around you that make them stand out?

What qualities would you like to develop or grow in yourself?

How have you built expertise or experience in your work?

4word™

Have you ever felt frustrated or impatient – that no one notices your value?

Huldah built her expertise and gained experience for a task that she was unaware that she would face. Has there been a time in your own life where God prepared you for a task and when faced with the task, you were ready to handle it?

Experience involves waiting. As you work and gain experience, what is your attitude towards the waiting? Are you impatient and wishing it away? Are you embracing the waiting and being all-in as you learn and work?

Do you ever struggle with knowing when and how to go outside of your job description? What can you learn from Huldah?

NOTES

PRAY

:: Pray for those you know in the midst of a reputational challenge. Ask God to work in their lives to renew them and grow their desirable qualities.

:: Ask God to reveal the qualities in you that are growing through your work.

:: Ask God for patience and diligence in continuing to grow while waiting.

:: Ask God for guidance to know when to go outside your job description.

NOTES

NOTES

4word

REFLECT

When things go wrong in life, are you tempted to give up all hope?

READ

:: 2 Kings 4

:: Romans 15:13

:: Psalm 18:28

:: Psalm 34:17-18

:: Luke 9:10-17

:: Mark 9:24

When you're in a crisis, to whom do you turn for help?

Why do you think the widow asked Elisha for help?

Notice how Elisha dealt with the widow's grief. What can we learn from his approach?

In difficult times, it is tempting to want to hand over all the responsibility to someone else to fix your problem. But Elisha made sure the widow kept the responsibility and worked to fix her problem. Have you ever experienced the healing power of work?

The widow had to trust Elisha and God. She didn't question the task assigned to her and obeyed with faith. Do you find yourself living in a conflicted state of doubt and belief? How can you resolve this tension?

Do you feel your house is empty? Take another look in your cupboard. What resources do you have to bring to the table?

Have you ever experienced a situation like the widow's? What did you give to God? How did He work with it?

4word

PRAY

NOTES

:: When faced with a difficult situation, ask God for humility to ask for help and for wisdom in choosing who to ask.

:: Ask God to reveal what you have to give when you feel that you have nothing left.

:: Thank God for the blessings you see in the midst of difficult situations.

:: Ask God to help you overcome your unbelief in difficult times.

5 Steps to Healing That We Can Learn From the Widow and Elisha

1. Ask for help, but don't give all of the responsibility to someone else.

2. Take inventory of what you have. What resources have you been given that you can use?

3. Once you have been given your plan, don't hesitate or ask questions before setting to work.

4. Trust God's plan and His direction.

5. Give the glory to God.

NOTES

REFLECT

Can you relate to Esther's hidden identity? Have you ever hidden your faith at work?

Have you ever found yourself in a high position but feeling alone and deserted like Esther? How do you handle being in a position where you don't feel like you belong?

Esther found herself in the right place at the right time to help her people. But she had to risk everything to do so. How would you have responded if you were Esther?

READ

:: Book of Esther

:: Romans 8:28

:: Philippians 2:13

:: Ephesians 2:10

:: Ecclesiastes 3:1

Esther risked her life to approach the king. What can we learn from her preparation before she entered the throne room?

What can we learn from her patience in preparing two banquets for the king and Haman?

Has God ever placed you in a position for a reason? Looking back, was it a position you sought or expected?

How did God use you for His purposes?

Esther used her authority to empower and honor the people. What does this teach us about her leadership?

PRAY

:: Ask God to use you in the positions He has placed you in.

:: Ask God for grace in the moments when you make mistakes.

:: Ask God to prepare you for His future plans for you.

5 Ways To Honor and Empower People Under Your Leadership

NOTES

:: Recognize the accomplishments of the people you lead.

:: Entrust your team with responsibilities.

:: Identify their gifts and talents and give them tasks that utilize those giftings.

:: Remember your own shortcomings and handle others' shortcoming with grace.

:: Speak encouraging words to your team members.

NOTES

NOTES

REFLECT

What are some of the stereotypes of working women today in the church?

In the professional world, what are some of the stereotypes of women in the church?

How does Proverbs 31 speak to both of these stereotypes?

READ

:: Proverbs 31

:: 2 Corinthians 3:4-5

:: 2 Corinthians 9:8

Do you feel like you have been targeted by these
stereotypes from your coworkers or fellow believers?

How have you responded to these stereotypes?

Have you ever confused excellence and perfection?

Do you agree that perfectionism can lead to the zero-sum
game? Explain.

4word™

Do you need to let go of your desire for perfectionism and seek excellence instead? What steps can you take to make that shift?

What talents do you have to put on the table?

Do you think it is possible to "have it all"? Is balance even a worthy goal? Why?

4word

What would it look like in your own life to stop juggling and start blending?

 NOTES

What can we learn from the character traits set forth in Proverbs 31?

How are you making sure your relationship with God doesn't get lost among the other parts of your life?

PRAY

:: Ask God to take away your desire for perfection and help you pursue excellence instead.

:: Ask God to reveal your talents and show you how to use them for His glory.

:: Ask God to help you find the right balance in your life.

:: Thank God for the different aspects of your life that He has blessed you with.

NOTES

NOTES

REFLECT

How did Mary's "credentials" uniquely qualify her to be the mother of Jesus?

READ

:: Luke 1 and 2

:: Luke 1:28-38

:: John 19:26-27

:: Luke 2:41-52

:: John 2:3-5

:: Jeremiah 29:11

How do you think you would you have responded to Gabriel if you were Mary?

Mary said yes to God, even though she lacked information and understanding. How does her attitude change your approach to daily work?

How much thought and importance do you place on your plans? How does this contrast with Mary's approach to plans?

Have you ever thought of Mary as a single mother? Does this help to appreciate the pressure and stress she must have encountered?

Mary does not require full understanding before she acts. How do the prerequisites for your actions compare to Mary's?

Do you need to relinquish your need for a road map about the future? How can you let go of this need and rely on God?

Do you tend to worry or do you tend to ponder? How have you seen these tendencies in your life?

Think about how you seek to gain influence in situations. How can you influence through a nudge instead of being overbearing?

Does greater pain lead to greater accomplishments in our work? Can you think of any examples?

NOTES

PRAY

:: Ask God to help you change your approach to your daily work so that you are open to His plans.

:: Ask God to relieve you of your need for a road map. Ask Him to help you trust His guidance.

:: Ask God to help you shift your thoughts from worrying to pondering.

:: Thank God for your work and the opportunities and plans He brings.

6 Lessons to Take Away from Mary's Life

NOTES

:: Don't overestimate your plans. Instead, underestimate them by being available.

:: Don't be afraid to say "Yes" to God.

:: Fulfill your responsibilities that arise, even the unexpected ones.

:: Understanding is not a prerequisite to action.

:: Ponder instead of worrying.

:: Blessings can come through pain.

NOTES

REFLECT

Do you feel like your amount of work causes trouble in your life?

Are you a multitaskaholic?

How does this affect the important relationships in your life?

How do distractions affect your daily work?

READ

:: Matthew 11:28-29

:: Ephesians 2:8-9

:: Luke 10:38-42

:: John 11:1-44

:: John 12:2

:: 2 Corinthians 3:18

4word

When is the last time you stopped to give your full attention to someone or something?

What step(s) could you take to minimize your distractions during the week? What would it look like to set aside your smartphone for a day (or part of a day)?

Martha worked to seek God's favor. Who are you working for? What are you trying to prove in your work?

Are you putting your work ahead of your heart?

Look at the contrast between Martha and Mary. Why was it so hard for Martha to sit at Jesus' feet? Why did it come so naturally for Mary?

Have you been working to earn God's favor? How does the truth that God's grace is a free gift change your priorities?

Read Matthew 11:28-29. What are some of the heavy burdens you carry?

Do you feel like you are carrying the burden alone? What burdens can you let go of and give to God?

NOTES

In what ways do you relate to the "Martha Syndrome"? With which symptom do you most identify?

Do you seek to find your significance in your work? How can you shift your perspective to find your significance in God?

4word™

Notice how Martha's faith grew and changed. What do you appreciate most about her story?

NOTES

PRAY

:: Thank God for His grace and the relief He offers when you are overwhelmed.

:: Ask God to help minimize the distractions in your life that divert your focus away from Him.

:: Ask God to release you from the burdens that weigh you down.

:: Ask God to help shift your perspective to find your significance in Him.

NOTES

Can you think of a modern-day Lydia?

:: Acts 16:13-15

:: Philippians 1:3-6

:: Philippians 4:3

:: Philippians 4:15-18

:: 2 Corinthians 9:6-7

What does Lydia teach us about being successful in faith and business?

Consider Lydia's conversion and decision to host the New Testament church in her home. What was she risking?

Have you had to adjust your priorities and resources for your faith? Have you given up your style? Why?

What can we learn about stewardship from the Philippian church?

How are you using the platform God has given you for Jesus?

Lydia's legacy lives through the church of Philippi. Consider your own legacy. What kind of mark do you hope to leave behind?

NOTES

PRAY

:: Thank God for both your faith and business.

:: Ask God to help you honor Him in both faith and business.

:: Ask God to help you be a good steward of the blessings He has given you.

:: Ask God to reveal to you what kind of legacy you are leaving.

4word

What are some of the traits that made Priscilla and Aquila a successful team?

:: Acts 18

:: Romans 16:3-5, 21

:: 1 Corinthians 16:19

:: Matthew 18:20

:: Matthew 19:26

How did they break the stereotypes of men and women working together in business?

What does it look like to be interdependent and not codependent?

If you are married, how would you characterize your relationship as compared to Priscilla and Aquila? What can you learn from Priscilla and Aquila's relationship?

What is it about work that enables us to really bond? Notice how Priscilla and Aquila bonded with Paul as they worked together. Have you ever experienced this type of relationship with your co-workers?

How can you improve your relationships with your co-workers?

Imagine constantly relocating your home and business. How do you think Priscilla dealt with this type of lifestyle?

How would you deal with this type of lifestyle?

What lessons can you take from Priscilla's life and apply to your own life?

PRAY

:: Pray for the relationships in your own life, both at home and at work.

:: Ask God how you can improve those relationships.

:: If you are married, pray for your marriage and ask God how you can work to improve the interdependence between you and your husband.

NOTES

4word

Have you ever felt undervalued or overworked? When?

READ

:: John 3:16

:: Mark 6:3

:: John 2:1-11

:: John 21:1-14

How does Jesus' work as a carpenter change your perspective?

How does your view of your work change knowing that God values your work?

Do you agree that modern women have avoided the
church based on the perception that work isn't valued?

How can we change this thinking?

Read John 3:16. Will you allow God to transform your
work?

PRAY

:: Thank God for giving us the example of Jesus as a worker.

:: Thank Him for valuing your work and ask Him to bless your work efforts.

:: Ask God to transform your perspective on your work.

Credits

Avery Dale

Susan DiMickele, Author of Working Women of the Bible

Diane Paddison, 4word Founder and CEO

Sandra Crawford Williamson, 4word COO

Katie Reiff, 4word Director

Betsy Gray Creative Group

NOTES

NOTES

NOTES

NOTES

NOTES

NOTES

Made in the USA
San Bernardino, CA
21 December 2017